Our Quivers:

Drawing Arrows From Fear

By:

Jorge Andres Rodriguez

Copyright © 2015 Jorge Andres Rodriguez
All rights reserved.
ISBN: 1499104545
ISBN-13: 978-1499104547

Table Of Contents

Fire Flies	6
Fabled	8
This Is Courage	9
Will-O'-The-Wisps	10
Wraiths In The "Wanted!" Posters	11
Shadowboxing With Satan	12
If God Exists	14
The Future	15
The Crimes We Commit	16
Lonely Thief	18
Gutting A Sinking Heart	20
All I See Is Black	22
The Fresh Scent Of Burning Flesh	24
All The World	28
Harm	29
Pyrecision	30
Rain, Rain Go Away	32
Nighttime Shade	34
Cardinal Directions	35
Animal Tactics	36
Titans Of Hearts Ne'er Barer	38
Abandoned Properties	40
Jailed Time	43
Infinity Combine	44
Low-lying Branches	46
The Best Bridges	48
Burning Bridges	49
Breathing: A Storm	50
Breathing The Storm	53
Masterful Transformations	55
Goldfist	56

Dust To Ice	58
Knives And Teeth	60
Born Cages	62
Blue Jay	63
Choke Ink	64
The Way Our Poems Change Us	65
Tampering With Camp	66
City Boy	67
The Innocence	68
The Youngest Courage	69
Claustrophobia..	70
July Twenty-Third	73
When A Boy Says I Love You	74
How You Make Love To A Woman	76
Subconscious Consent	78
That's The Dream	80
Old Souls, Young Fun	82
Lottery	83
Once Crumbled, Now Golden	84
Nova Altitude	85
Temple And Vessel	86
Whistles	87
Grand Illusionist	88
For Sake Of Solving Forsaken Puzzles	89
Letters: Part V	90
Letters: Part VI	91
Unsent Letters: Part II	92
Just A Reminder	94
The Only Soul Left Unscathed	96
Trials To Tame	98
It's Only In My Nature To Love	99
Long Walks..	100
Steadfast	101
It's Easy To Love You So	102

Atone	104
Crisp Leaves	105
The Vices Of Asking Axes For Advice	106
The Reasons We Read	108
Crop Circles	110
Nights	113
Arms Like Iron Maidens	114
Dam, That's Deep	115
The Reacher	116
The Settler	117
Hex	119
Nemesis	120
Phoenix	121
Frostwalker	122
Skypouncer	123
Tangerine Mint Gimlets	124
Tender	126
Sundays	128
The Teachings Of A True Father	129
Unconquerable	130
Royalty In Nosebleed Seats	132
Cease The Day, Carpe Noctem	134
Conducting Chaos	135
Only If I Tremble	136
The Lights Tremble	137
Serpentine Skylines	139
Incandescence	140
Horizons Drawn Like Henna	142
Feathered Moon	144
Shattered Suns	145
Accuracy	146
Purposeful Impact	147
Rough Roses	149
Cinnamon Oceans	150

Fire Flies

Our pupils eclipse the same blazing
Sun straddling the horizons of the skies overhead,
Our irises connect cloud canvases
With crepuscular rays,
Our blinding eyes remind others why it is not
Wise to have staring contests with us.
Our heraldic crests remain stitched behind
Our open eyelids as opposed to badges of
Honor on our closed chests,
Our messages reside in the envelopes of
Our untamed flames,
Our dreams and desires burn like
Hell-lit lanterns in dark rooms.
Our valor is the harbinger for boon sparks,
Our hope ignites our souls so they may
Dance like solar storms,
Our passion protects our hearts day and night like
Terracotta army spirits armed with
Spears, shields and swords.
Our fire flies so as to incinerate those who insinuate
Those who catch fireflies are passing time like
Dynamite but my glowing fingertips trace the light
Trails of my dynamism like dousing pendulums.
Our smoke tendrils signal our comfort with being an
Object of combustion,
Our eyes are the only warning you get before we
Vaporize your existence to soot,
Our eyes can turn Giants, Gods and Golems to
Ash with ease before they get consumed and

Buried beneath the boots of vigorous Sun stars
costumed in bone-tight suits.
Our eyes may cage our flames but, remember,
    It is, simply, not out of fear,
        But mercy.

Fabled

I am the fabled definition
Of garden weeds.
Unsightly and pesky,
Untamed and unrelenting,
I am the ugly truth and reminder.
I am the smudges across
The world's rose colored glasses.
I am the fabled definition
Of garden weeds.
Creeping and strangling,
Preaching and mangling,
I am still the child of nature,
An equally honorable creation of beauty.
You can rip me from the ground
In hopes that I will
Die in silence but I have my
Own deep-reaching roots.
I was seeded an honest poet.
I do not need the same
Latticework naive roses are
Espaliered to climb.
I do not need the same
Trellis to stand as my spine.
All I need is silence in this garden so
We may all hear every
Message carried in the
Prayers of the weak,
Whispers of the strong and
Songs of the proud.

This Is Courage

Aim your arrows high -
Your efforts reach across
Our Father Sky
As if they were shooting
For far past the Moon,
Landing in the safety net of stars
Wrapped in the comforting truth
Like cocoons concealing
Beautiful butterflies bound
To shed the shell by noon.
Drawing arrows from the
Quiver in our Hearts,
We are all just aiming for Greatness
But
Trembling in fear.
Surviving the tests of time
Have become the greatest
Factors in determining
If we truly value our Lives
And, if so, why it is that some
Of us sit idly by
On the leaves
We can't seem to leave
When we were given
Wings to fly.

Will-O'-The-Wisps

Charging through crowded roads like being
Out for blood in the thick of the woods,
I am traveling down the wrong path.
Will-O'-The-Wisps call out to me and
Beg that I do not hit the brakes.
Will-O'-The-Wisps call out to me and
Let me know that, though I am angry,
I am seeing red because
I am speeding down the
Wrong side of the road.
Drunk driving gave
Road reflectors life in the
Instant I could have taken my own.
Will-O'-The-Wisps,
I am not entirely sure they do not exist,
However,
I know, now, to steer clear of
The embers burning in
The bottom of bottles.

Wraiths In The "Wanted!" Posters

We smite our futures with
Intensive vigilance so as to
Persuade regrets to cower away
In their covert veil of naivety.
We serve justice with the fury
Of a thousand vendettas attacking and
Relieving themselves all at once.
These wars we wage against
Two-faced demons
Will never reach a resolution.
It's hard to take the right course of action
When we are too scared to face
Or even identify the true worst
Of our blood-born enemies -
What they are weak to is
Close to little known to us,
What they look like resembles
Our own flesh and bone.
So, what if these holy wars
To relinquish mistaken sins and
Accidental evils are our
Ways of realizing these demons
Look much like our own angels.
What if our demons looked
Exactly like the heroes
We imagined ourselves to be.

Shadowboxing With Satan

The fight in my chest was
Headlined in the papers as
"Underdog versus the Paid Pied Piper"
I married the commitment to
Conquer the fear,
So as I stood in the ring
Shadowboxing with Satan,
He learned my fists were
Laden with hatred.
It was exactly what he
Expected and Wanted.
I couldn't stand becoming a
Slave to the ignorant arrogance.
In every good man there is some evil -
There are ounces of vanity
In every last drop of confidence
Just the same.
A bullet is still a bullet
No matter what it is made of but
I chose to be the one that never harms,
The one that never gets locked and
Loaded in the barrel of the gun.
I stood in my corner and
Never set a foot further than
The initial battle stance.
I needed not to make an
Advance on the trap;
To not run directly into
The palm of crushing misfortune's hands.

Tantalized and Teased,
Tormented and Taunted,
The provocation haunted the
Grounds in the peripherals of my imagination.
My mind traveled to off and far away places,
A perspective that allowed me to see
The things that appear to be our biggest
Hassles become the smallest of troubles
With some distance between us and
Such hurdles that cloud our vision and judgment.
Fear is merely a human construct for
Doubting our own bravery and strength.
I stood shadowboxing with Satan and soon
I learned all that meant was
That I was only shadowboxing.

If God Exists

If God exists I must thank him
For the lessons he taught me.
Although I was handed calamities
When I pleaded for
Patience and strength,
I realize now there is little
Difference between the
Significance of those gifts.

The Future

What a cruel game,
The unknown.
Our nerves shake,
Shivering bones.
I'm afraid to have
My future told for
I can only think of no
Other way I'd live
But never taking chances and
Never wanting love -
Because mistakes are our
Hardest, most shattering lessons.

The Crimes We Commit

We could be off so far worse.
How lucky are we that our
Tragedies can fit on the tips of our tongues.
We tend to send search parties out for our voices
That have never gone missing,
We turn ourselves to victims to
See who will care enough
To come running through the
Imaginary burning houses
That exist in the basements of
Our figments of imagination.
We could drown in our own lives but
Can't use the lessons to douse our searing fears.
Instead, we drop the glass cup
That is either half-filled or half-empty while another
Person is dying of dehydration
With the hope just to sip from it.
We flail in our mind's oceans,
Scared to death to find the answers
That haunt and hunt these waters like Sharks -

"Why does this always happen to me?"

We need to ask ourselves better questions -

"Why can't we man-up and stand up
Out from the ripples in the kiddy pool?"
"Why can't we gather ourselves together
To mount a chance of pulling through?"

*"Why can't we understand it's really not that difficult,
If my heart can pump blood through twelve thousand miles
Of winding roads that encircle my body,
If my lungs can draw breath in seventeen thousand to
Thirty thousand times a day through centuries,
Why can I conjure the will from a couple of small
efforts to keep fighting?"*

The crimes we commit,
That we are continuously guilty of,
Are the acts of giving up and never,
Even remotely,
Coming close enough to
Walk the fine line of our own limits.

Lonely Thief

A poor boy.
Hand me downs and
Broken toys,
A smile just the same.
It swayed from cheek to cheek
To turn away from
Making complaints but
See-saws are never fun with sadness.
I never saw the ups in life,
Nor the birthdays that brought me joy.
The money tucked in those birthday
Cards were dealt to the hands of my parents.
I forgot about it.
A poor boy.
Girls in school scoffed at me and
Applauded the three boys who
Tormented me because I was nerdy.
I didn't wear Jordans or Converse,
I wore Sketchers and bruises.
I wore sadness like it was a fashion.
I wore tears like the invincible, and often
Imaginary, somethings in my eye.
I wore depression like it was awkward to be alive.
A poor boy.
My image flipped so many times
I started to look like catalogs for the egos
A Schizophrenic had in mind.
I wore my hair gelled down,
Gelled up, combed sideways,

Shaved, long, frizzy and spiked.
I edited myself to be what others
Thought would look acceptable in their eyes.
I chased my shadow wishing to only
Capture and strangle it.
I chased my shadow because it proved
I was still living.
A poor boy.
I blamed my pain on the
Actions of others and
Amounted my self-worth to
How much I was liked.
I realized...
I finally realized...
I was only poor in loving myself.
I was only poor because
I'd given myself no value.
Poor Boy.

Gutting A Sinking Heart

She asked "Honestly, can you
Tell me why you hate me?"

My mind flies into hyper-speed
Traveling through years of depression,
But how the fuck do you answer a
Question like that without sounding
Like you mean it?
I feel the hate,
I don't necessarily want the hate.
I want to forgive,
I don't necessarily feel the forgiveness.

How do you place your hands
Around the throat of a Ghost?
How do you slide nooses around the necks of
Haunting spirits without catching your own?
How can you claim you'll bury the hatchet
When it always ends up in my back?
How do you shift shivering chills through my bones
Without ever being around?

I sigh "It's been years and
I've never said I hate you, that is,
It's just that when I think of talking to you
My heart thinks of why it prefers
To be left alone -
One sided conversations epitomize
My childhood."

I tear up or maybe
I tear myself up;
Sometimes it's hard to differentiate
Between the ways that I feel.

She says "No one is prepared to be
The perfect mom – are you
Waiting for me to die?"

My mind jumps the gun.
I wanted a Mother, not the perfect mom.
I want to really be loved, to actually be loved.
I wanted a best friend, not static silence.
I can't stand stagnant waters, and Yet...

"...No Mom, I'm just waiting for you to start truly wanting to live."

All I See Is Black

He said *"All I see is black."*

You can not expect to be a Jack of all trades
Without also being a Master of none.
You can not find life's answers in Clubs or in
Searching the graves your Spades have dug.
I understand the frustration,
Letting bygones be bygones
Comes at quite the cost but
Mining for someone's Heart
When your at war with the World and Yourself
Doesn't always pan out the
Promise of the blood Diamonds
You plan to use to pay due for the
Weapons you've needed
In separating your Heart from the hurt.
You're not alone on the front lines of this war
But you're the only one that still wagers you'll
Walk away from the settling smoke a victor of battle.
Lay down your worried mind,
Drop your turrets and ammo,
Remove your finger from the trigger,
Wipe the sweat from your brow and
The blood from your shoulders,
You've slaughtered the entrails inside your skull,
Collect your ideas and the soul that's been scattered -
We believe you, Antonio,
The battle's been won for awhile and long, long ago.
We still remember your smile.

Don't Flush what Royal blood courses
Straight through your veins,
You're one-of-a-kind,
A freshly fired gun with precision aim,
You're a smoking ace.
We are a Full House, with a fire escape.
We were gifted The Flop, Three sisters,
You were The Turn, Fourth born, and
I am The River, Last of the womb.
Together, there are lessons to learn.
Our sisters tell us to make better choices
Than what they have so we don't fall short,
You were suppose to make the halting realization
That we weren't given much and it is no one's fault,
I am the collector of tears, I hear
All of your voices and cries,
Believe me, it kills me, but sometimes
I fumble over the receding waves of the tide.
We are all struggling to make it out of our own fights,
Five of us were gifted purpose and at this point
Losing one will become the literal strikes against us
In this game of H.O.R.S.E. versus Life.
So to stop seeing black, won't you open your eyes?
Hands in, it's our turn to shoot the dice.
It's your turn to move.

The Fresh Scent of Burning Flesh

There was a fire in his eyes -
One that consumed his heart,
Peace of mind and
The flashes of memories
Of how he was forced
To leave his childhood behind
Far too early on.
There was a yearning in his
Anxious hands to make mends.
He understood he could only hope for a better life
If he let his efforts that wouldn't bend
Lead the way.
There was a patient, confident, adult
Sound in his voice -
The facade he put forth to null
The echoes of the cries
He hid as a boy.
There was an anger in his soul -
One that he just couldn't let go.
His future had been foretold
By the habits his parents had grown.
He refused to let his own
Story be written -
A strike to the windpipe
Like his quill had been silenced
And his creativity smitten.
These pages were no ones but his
To fill with his meaning of
Life and things like

"This is how the story goes" and
"When I was just eight years old,
A strange man came back from jail
And expected things to return to the norm;
Nearly knocked down the damn door."
His mind would undergo an endless cycle
Of underestimation and vexation,
Confidence and Doubts,
Brutal bouts with his imagination and
The difficulty he found in
Turning lemons to lemonade;
The lessons in first bettering himself.
Beat on by Bullies,
Parents abusing the kindness,
He wondered why he was always met with injustice.
The drive that fueled him
Short-circuited at his core.
Electric cords wrapped around
An ego, like exposed wires and
When met with a source of running water
Sent surging shocks that surgically
Slashed at his spine.
His tears and frustration blinded the eye of reason
But he managed to survive.
After a while, he put it together -
Results are conjured by the effect of the
Amount of effort you exert.
He stood in a desolate desert or He stood on an Island,
His surroundings became the mirrors
Of his own perspective.
He felt there was no motive or He felt he had life left,

His fight became the bottle that carried his message.
He made it to Main land or He died trying,
The progress he made was a
The sight of seagulls to a doomed ship.
But call it a gambit, he laid his words to sea.
He put his weaknesses to the currents
So someone in the present or future
Could see of what people mean
When they speak of the gift that
"The consequences whether good or bad
Even the least of them are far reaching."
Whether he lit up his own heart or
He moved a generation to action,
It's a mystery left to the waves that
Ought to be discovered when
High tide completely finishes intercostal retracting -
When Ancient Oceans stop breathing.
He put a new meaning to having a bright mind.
The reach of the smoke made curious folk wonder
If the fire prevailed and if so,
What it actually looked like beyond its veil.
His body went up in ruins from bending
Backwards to help others.
None of us were meant to contort our bodies
So far as to sweep the floorboards with our hair.
Call his significance as inspiring as the
Glum myth of Atlantis,
After all a Pirate in his ship is nothing but
A drop compared to the infinite reach of the Ocean.
But would it be fair to dock
Every individual drop away from its home?

If every drop were placed away on their own,
Wouldn't our story just be a collection of
Sob-story puddles
Instead of the magnificent history of a
Collective whole?

All The World

We are never quite comfortable in our skin.
We all deny that we have secrets we keep in
And maybe we are right.
We bury ourselves in the latest fashions.
Perhaps, we bury our true selves
In our secrets just the same.
So if this truly is the case,
Drinking with our Sins,
Applauding our Imperfections,
Confessing our Demons and
Dancing with our Skeletons,
Must be the only ways to parade
Out of our dark closets
Naked and free from the worry
Of the stammers and mistakes
We have made on this stage named Life.
There is no dress rehearsal for our Acts and Scenes.
Without improvisation we may confuse it
For a scripted play when all it is
Is a show of facing fear with might,
Capturing our dreams with
Our will to achieve and
Forcing the Monarchs that
Tease our stomachs with their wings,
Making us shy and queasy,
To leave in permanent fleeting migration.

Harm

Destroy what destroys you -
Thus, I am no more.
Two negatives make a positive -
Are you sure it is not worse,
Are you sure it is not nothing at all?
Fight fire with fire -
I'm afraid I may get burnt,
I'm afraid I may turn to ash,
But
I'm afraid far more to escape,
I'm afraid I may have worth.

Pyrecision

A Devil's Advocate,
I count the large sums of precious moments
I, accidentally, missed on my abacus and
Dismiss the narrow-shortsightedness as
The foolishness of a Pessimistic Optimist.
I realized revenge is better served as
A torrid dish for those with sub-zero hearts,
To rid of those whose passion will never be a match
For the ambition and pride I take in my art.
The interest people have invested has gathered
Momentum as quickly as an unexpected flash mob.
My words cause spontaneous human combustion,
I am the ignition, they are the spark.
I've done time for the crimes I've never committed
And gotten away with murder
Without ever being a person of interest.
If I was worried about being caught by suspicion
The bodies would've been hidden.
Now, some think they're psychics
Because I've had my palms red,
I'm as guilty of Sin and Selfishness
As all of you who think you're in good standing
By admitting them in Confessionals while
Expecting to be automatically forgiven.
You're the Lord's prophet?
Well, I am personified Arson.
Our sons will profit from ceasing to confuse
The righteous path with general reciprocity and
Following fate through ignorant blindness.

Our sons will profit from excusing the great
Trespassings against them with forgiveness and
Welcoming even their enemies with
True acts of kindness.
If today I knocked down the Churches walls,
The Sun would reveal maggots,
The decay of strung-up puppets.
People, nowadays, hold up their savior for
His face value, like monetary currency, and
Have tantrum fits when someone challenges it.
I don't have to hold up any
Individual to the true gracious Light
To test whether they're counterfeit.
I see right through them.
I hold up this disconnected dedication to God
To gift the courtesy that the truth's transparency
Demonstrates no one is any longer a true believer.
I pray for a day when everyone is more focused on
Kindling and acting on actions as opposed to
Collecting the word of mouth.
I wish that we may, just, be able to
Capture the crown sitting in the Clouds overhead.

Rain, Rain Go Away

Reaching for opportunity,
Patiently awaiting my chance,
The passing of storms
Present hidden weapons and gems.

Rainbows follow them to
Ensure dark times are met
With a new day's Iron Fist.

Capturing the colors
Of every kind of jewel,
The Bow to shoot
Our Sharp Efforts
Into the mysterious moon
Sends them speeding past
The secretive storm with
The combined power and agility
Of Javelins and Maces,
Arrows and Swords.

I faced the facts.
I messed up miserably and
Long have I paid for my mistakes.

But, I hurried to the hurricane,
Horrified by the wails that outweighed
The heavy cries of a pod of Whales,
Like I was swallowed up inside
The belly of the beast.

I could not retreat.
I stared down the
Eye of the storm and
Swore to myself that
I would not know defeat.

So as I woke from my daydream,
The voice of the rainbow
Traveled the distance,
Winds whispered in speech,
"Lay down your arms, Victor,
The battle's been Won."

And to this day,
I'd like to think it enjoys being hung,
Upside down, Smiling at me.

Because I've learned that
A change in the natural occurrence of things
Proves dark times are met with the light
Of brighter days,
That we're not given what we can't handle
And that even when we lose our way,
We can find comfort knowing
Storms will always rage and
Our efforts will always reign.
Rain, go away.

Nighttime Shade

We were Poison.
Where two wrongs have
Never made a right,
Was I a fool for assuming we
Could prove to be potions
Capable of ridding each
Others potent habit of
Poaching hearts?
Was I a fool for not
Locking jaws with the beast;
Resting my trust in between your
Death-dealing, razor-like teeth and
Saliva-soaked, foam-filled mouth?
Was I a fool for hesitatingly wishing
That hope could heal the hurt?
Surely, I was, you'd concur,
Rabid animals have no feelings
To spare while trying to survive the hunt.

Cardinal Directions

I, too, know what it is like
To not be strong enough.
I have dragged like a parachute
Against an unrelenting Wind.
I have drained myself skipping steps in stride
On the climb up descending escalators.
I have backstroked and breaststroked,
Butterfly-stroked and doggy-paddled hopelessly,
Struggling against the currents and rip tide.
I have looked you straight dead in the eyes,
While death had manifested in your eyes,
Battling my Heart to just, simply,
Turn the other way.
Though, with what but trust and hope
Do we hold that compass in our chests.
We all allow our hearts to lead us,
Even if we know it may guide us by the
Promise of silver light
Straddling the edge of the cliffside.

Animal Tactics

Like Great White Sharks in the Shallows,
Like Rabid Wolves at the Gates,
Like Crowned Eagles circling the sight of Prey,
Taunting teasingly, I will wait.

Like Gods atop the Gallows,
Like Jesters in the Jungle,
Like Sleeping Giants in Narrow Alleyways,
Like Trust, Old Friend, Misplaced.

Careless in your cluelessness,
Your battle with immaturity rings loudly
Like a rattlesnake.

Like Komodo Dragons and Inland Taipans
Playfully patient in
Their perilous practices,
Like Bush Elephants
Barreling and bum-rushing
Every advance to assault and
Insult their intelligence,
I will wait until we've
Closed our distances and
Hoist your remains on the
Tusks of Vengeance,
Bearing your Blood on my
Coat of Fur
That stands my
Coat of Arms at War.

I will flay your existence,
Wear the threads so thin,
Your frail flesh unravels,
A heart falls untangled
To the dust and gravel,
A grave so shallow
Even your slippery serpent body
Couldn't make its own ghost
Turn in it.

Titans Of Hearts Ne'er Barer

Hibernating with our minds
Trapped in the hindsight of our pasts,
Even the thickest coats of fur
Couldn't shelter us from the turmoil
Of revisiting our mistakes.
We should forbear from this burden.
Bearers of times wounds,
We've never stood barer.
Second's sands sink salaciously,
Sins stripped of anything worldly,
Whispering sweet somethings that could
Only ever offer Hell.
While they settle down in their citadels,
Denizens defend their dens, again,
Against the anonymous
Threats of animosity.
Long have we been driven by the
Rage embedded in the messages
Left painted on the walls of our caves.
Ancestral tools for the
Ridding of haunting banes
Became the rituals of learning to
Free ourselves from blame
As our tender paws turned away.
It was only in facing the blizzard,
The harsh breaths of temperatures
Tempered with mirroring contempt,
That we could stand the
Myriad of didactic winds.

Play-dead tactics couldn't stand apart
From the antics of our nature.
Barehanded choke holds
Became those strategies that controlled
The volume of the voices that longed
To screech and scold us for
Reliving the pain,
For that habit has grown old.
We had to realize that
We are Titans,
Boulder-bodied behemoths
With a power so berserk
The ground of heaven and earth shook,
Erupting with cries of relief.
Though, once tattered with age,
Bruised, beaten and broken,
When I rise,
Enemies will be forced to flee
Because, like a cold,
I can guarantee you'd agree
You will never
Have wanted to catch me.

Abandoned Properties

A House was just walls and beams
We added to our collections of
Barricades and Pillars meant
To shut everyone else out.
Doors slamming and music blasting
Became the ways silenced hard feelings
Decided to express themselves.

A Home was where our
Trust and Doubts mingled.
We could lay our
Heads down on worry and
Wake reassured by our dreams.

I've grown so tired of
Duct-taping windows shut and
Using Krazy glue to hold
Shattered Good China pieces together.
I've grown mad on my own enough.

I've grown so tired of hearing
The sinks and old pipes mock
My tears, cries and fumbling lungs.

I've grown so tired of making
Rusty nails and thumbtacks
The arms for which our
Family pictures are hung.

I've grown so tired of this broken house and
I've grown so sick of how it
Mirrors the lack of progress and growth.
Shattered reflections give apparitions like us
Seven years to hail hallowed Mary or
Gamble with the Devil for better luck.

I've grown so tired of silly excuses.
Simple solutions can't subdue
The certain insecurity granted by the
Things we ought to improve on.

Sugar-coating unhappiness, at best,
Looks like a face canvased by
Running make-up masking
Tea-bagged troubled eyes,
Sinking crescent lips,
Feverish cheeks and the words
"I'm Okay" that seem to choke
As they trip over clunky sniffles.

There comes a point where
Ordinary remedies can't make
Quick fixes of permanent problems.

We try to stretch apologies over chasms
Of voids of broken hearts,
Mistrust and lost hope.
Sometimes kisses and bandages
Just can't mend our broken bones.

Sometimes hearing someone
Say "Sorry" sounds like the easiest
Way they can get on with
Selfishly forgiving themselves.

Home is where the heart is,
So while we will age and crumble down,
Remember your actions and words
Can crush an others world -
Thus, we shouldn't throw stones
While we all live under the roof
Of the same glass house.

Jailed Time

The thing about prison gates
Is that they don't tell you
They trap everyone behind bars
With their true selves.
The thing about prison gates
Is that they don't tell you
They will drag every inmate's family
In along with them.
Jail time -
Everyone is on the inside.
The thing about prison gates
Is that they don't warn you that
The walls are never convicted of
Bloody murder for brutally torturing the
Minds of those encaged.
The thing about prison gates
Is that they find ways to
Create an eternal void
In the chests of many
So no member of the family
Can reach them even when
They yell into the darkness.
Jail time -
Everyone serves a sentence.
The reminders of all those affected,
Individual charges,
Each its own punishing sentence.
The thing about prison gates
Is that everyone is on the inside.

Infinity Combine

We meet,
You leave,
You left,
We met.
Repeat
To free
Your hands
Stained red.

We met,
I leave,
I left,
We met.
Life gives
So we can
Gift life
Right back.

I'm sorry for
Doing time,
Instead of
Taking the time.

We leave,
I work,
You Work,
We meet.

We forgive,
We understand,
We never see
Eye to eye.
Literally.

I think you think,
It's time to meet,
Again,
And finally,
Eight-year old me agrees.

Low-lying Branches

The way a baby tries to
Cry his Mother's name -
Is it a phase we expect to see elsewhere?
A seedling hangs to its parents all it can
Before it finds itself parted away
Like a break up following
The shake of hands.
But only by the sleight of hand
Does it begin to have a
Slight chance to address hope -
We all have to adventure
Far from the sight of home.
Wishes to grow big and
Wishes to grow tall,
It thinks of how home sick
It'll grow later on.
Ever wonder why trees
Reach out far and wide?
It isn't just a show of pride,
And I might be going out on a limb,
But would it be
Entirely impossible, implausible,
To believe these lower-lying branches
Are just trying to
Remember their roots
In the same way we try to
Remember our kin?
Wood, Fur or Feathers for skin,
We're all still Natures' children within.

We all reach for our Mothers.
We all know we still need them.
Their roots reach far further
For no other than the core of Gaia.
It's not Nature versus Nurture,
Nature is a nurturer,
At the Center, our hearts are homes
That were meant to offer comfort.
Once kids are ready to be on their own,
They'll drop like apples
But holding onto them too long
Will only make of them
A lump upon a log and
Allowing them to leave in the dead of night
Will only stunt their chance to ripen.

The Best Bridges

Knots of friendship,
Nods of approval,
Jesters set aside their jokes for
Gestures as serious as
Tears cried at a funeral.
There's far more behind a handshake,
A bond of trust and happiness within.
The Grim Reaper's touch doesn't
Have an edge
Over the combined
Power of friends.
Grasps of strength,
So when gasps of
Discomfort and distress set in,
True friends will know that
They've got each others backs forever,
Never turning a shoulder,
Never giving a back to the other.
Face facts,
Allies face the enemy's
Front-lines together.

Burning Bridges

You can't rebuild bridges
If you stand on those still burning
But ruin can cease if forgiveness
Is allowed to extinguish the fires,
Casting them down from
Causing any further damage.

Breathing: A Storm

I was losing my mind.

Mental instability strikes like fangs and
Sinks into our dreams and visions
Like snake-eyed migraines injecting
Vials of vile poison.
I wish I could say Goodbye to Hell on
This Earth and Hello to Goodbye,
I wish I could remember
That all is fair in love and war
And sometimes
That means everything is fair
In love and war.
I wish I would remember why
These battles are waged.
While time is laid to waste,
Lives are wagered every day
With little to gain.
Most of the time I think about the
Memories that could have been made
But their images are just as vague as those
Killed in action are hard to remember by name.
Wars are won the instant we stop playing
Pretend with our shadows,
Making something out of nothing
Like moving silhouettes on walls
Bright lights and fingers folded for models.
Making martyrs of unfounded heroes,
If I listened to the voices

That creep around corners with
Dirty daggers in my mind,
Maybe I'd realize they're reminders
Of learning to disregard our pasts
To leave the worst of ourselves behind.
"No man left behind" never felt any more inaccurate.
I've shed the skins of a thousand dead layers
In the most innocuous and murderous of ways.
I've held myself captive like a menacing medic
Forcefully peeling back the scabbed edges
That festered with rotting pain.
I've fought back the enemy lines,
To recapture myself from the grips of sure dismay.
I've lost and found myself so many
Times along the way
That I'm only one to blame.
I'm the one always ready to lock and aim
But find myself catching my own bullets to the brain.
Onomatopoeia makes a punch to the face sound
Like an acronym that seems to entertain;
Prisoner Of War.
I wish there was a label for the failure to escape
The cycle of Russian roulette like
Rushing through revolving doors.
Remember, you only need one
Madman in a chamber before
Zealous insanity takes over and
Begins to dismember you whole.
I've signed peace treaties with myself but
I'll be the death of myself.
I've protested my fear, it's threatened to kill,

But it always seems like it's in the one in control.
The ghost town where I reside
Stands in unsung echoes of battlefields
That once rung with battle cries.
If I chose to run and hide,
Shelter from the sands that pelt
Skins that felt like raw leather hide,
Would being missing in action
Grant me some clarity of peace of mind?
Or would Miami still remind me of
It's like to be lost inside?
The battlegrounds bound inside our skulls
Fight round after round,
With machine gun turrets, rounds after rounds,
Victories and losses come in turns, round and around,
Dulled knives, doubts that serve no point,
I've altogether come full-circle like a
Ritualistic and sacrificial cult -
Insanity is defined by the repetition of our actions
With the expectation of different results;
A far shot chance, miraculously occult.

Breathing The Storm

For those suffering through
What they suppose is a
Suffocating curse that is
A pounding heartbeat,
That feeling stuck in your throat
Is the voice of every soul
Awaiting their turn to breathe the storm.
Not always will Lilacs
Address a dreamer's hopes but
Surreal Spring will always offer
The scent of the poet's jasmine.

Not always will the winds
Blow in your favor.
Sometimes you may sail
Upon a sea breeze,
Sometimes you may drift
In the comfort of zephyrs,
Sometimes you may travel
With tail winds at your back,
Sometimes you may encounter
Your own demons and dust devils,
Sometimes gales and gusts will make
You want to bail and bust,
Sometimes you may have to tackle
The headwinds to keep getting up,
Sometimes you may have to seek
Refuge inside yourself
To avoid being swept away by tornadoes,

Sometimes your lungs may
Drown in the onslaught of
Unforgiving whirlwinds and windstorms.
Sometimes the same winds that lift
Your spirits are those to let you down.

But, if we can surround ourselves with
Good company, those who may
Bring both fun and drama,
But, if we can indulge in the material
Luxuries of life, those that may
Bring both joy and greed,
Why can't we surround ourselves
With the different extremes, and the
Shades in between, of the
Winds that always
Offer to fill our lungs with either
Happiness or Hope,
Life or Courage,
Wisdom or Resilience?
Suffocating is our own doing.
Suffocating is our own
Way to resist learning lessons.
Breathing the storm grants the
Privilege to gasp for fresh air.

Masterful Transformations

Our bruises sat like soil,
Enriched by the life cycles of lessons
And repetitions that had died there.
Our scars still spill like open wounds,
Open earth split by piercing pickaxes
And rusted shovels searching for prospects.
Our future blooms like meadows of fresh flowers or
Evergreen forests when we learn to let go
And grow with time.
It's just that our life force remembers what it is
Like to hurt the most under the surface but
Dresses our skin in silk river streams and
Rolling hills of potential mountain peaks.
This is the way it speaks.
This is how we let what is underneath
Fuel our freedom and
Turn our woes and wounds
To beauty.

Goldfist

Strong hands have sat on the edge.
Like my back, they bend
At every point they get to assist.
Wielding razors,
My raw wrists, still healing,
Cry the blood for tears they've shed.
I've been there.
I've taken shortcuts dragging
Long cuts through there.
I await the day I swing
My fist at the boulder
We've been baring.
I need to see burdens lifted -
Relieved when those in need
Recount the times they
Believed in something.
I need to see the
Gold veins run like
An open tab to rid bitter tastes and
Sip sweet life up like rum.
How long does it take to realize
A fortune's been won when
One's been gifted a life more valuable
Then monetary wealth to be struck?
We raise pickaxes to pry pieces of
Prosperous dreams from
Our own minds and
Expect to reap immediate
Success for our lives.

We must chisel and polish these tunnels
That are home to our sanity.
We must stop scratching at the doors,
Like wild animals in captivity.
We must free ourselves
From self-doubt's slavery.
Our hearts were not meant
To be hellishly harvested,
Our minds were not meant
To be meticulously mutilated,
Our bodies were not meant
To be barbarously burdened.
Our existence was not meant
To be overlooked by
Offenses or imperfections.
We are suppose
To triumph
Over disastrous consequences.

Dust To Ice

Confidence came in healing
Those who had fallen as well,
Back to whole hearts -
Escaping the lingering damage that
Has left my empathy in ruin,
Turned to disassociation.
Dust to ice.
Weighing worth became
Harder every day.
While my hands could nurse
The down-and-outs,
They served no good
To my own rebuilding.
Second thoughts and doubts
Sunk in at the wrong times;
Like a mistimed alarm in
The middle of the night,
Like I love you's on first dates
Like break ups at wedding
Like laugh attacks at funerals
Like expelling blood
From broken wrists
As a consequence of
Wanting to see what happens
There if I pressed down and
Dragged a blade effortlessly
Sharpened by self-hatred,
Like losing your job for being late
Like a flat tire on the interstate,

As I was trying to rest my worry,
As I was trying to express my relief,
As I was celebrating futures,
As I was admiring death and life,
As I was confusing being numb for grief,
As I was rushing from one job to another,
As I was driving distracted, jumping curves,
As I was crashing into brick walls of fear.
I fixed others problems
To avoid fixing my own
It was easier that way.
It was easy to label it as
Wanting to be but being
Inept to become.
It was easy to say that
I wanted to,
But so much harder to actually,
Change.
It was so difficult getting better.

Knives And Teeth

A light burns in the
Deepest reaches of my veins.
Shining through my scars,
It trembles violently like
Earth tremors echoing through
The great fissures of my indecisiveness.
Conspiring dreams counsel suffocation so
I find inspiration in the night terrors
That haunt what little
Slumber I manage to get.
Knives crash into my mouth,
My teeth ache like
Shooting stars crumbling
Under the weight of the
Ghosts that ride them.
I move silently through my day but
That does not mean that
I am without noise and worry.
Reckless clatter clutters the
Space between the
Ideas of my crimson crown and
The potential embedded in the
Trenches of my fingerprints.

I am always running
Against the landslide of emotion.
My depression dismantles my
World from beneath me
Like I am the house too

Close to the edge and
It is the mudslide that does
Not care who I am or
That I am a veteran of
World War What's-going-on-in-my-head.
Or maybe I am the mudslide -
A substance so undesirable
With disgusting texture,
The singularity of gloomy inconsistency,
A cold lump of dirt mixed
With salty tears,
The most unstable and
Incompetent building block,
And my depression is the
House sitting atop.
Sometimes I try to balance myself
By not making any sudden moves
But then, once again, the light comes
Burning through.
Underneath, I could be a Volcano.
I was asleep before but now
I'm gradually warming up
To being able to feel the
Fury of this fiery mantle plume.
I'm ready to let my heart
Erupt and run its course
To brush fingertips
With the mud.

Born Cages

We've lost ourselves;
Our souls to our pride
Our pride to our jealousy
Our jealousy to our reasoning
Our reasoning to our emotions
Our emotions to our brains
Our brains to our hearts
Our hearts to our doubts
Our doubts to our sanity
Our sanity to our confidence
Our confidence to our flesh
Our flesh to our insecurities
Our insecurities to our old flames
Our old flames to our hindsight
Our hindsight to our regrets
Our regrets to our growth
Our growth to our minds
Our minds to our Time
Our Time to our questions
Our questions to our answers
Our answers to our purpose
Our purpose to our blindness.

Blue Jay

It is none but the bird that rises
To the most frightening of heights
With, both, belief and wind
Beneath its wings that
Triumphs over the
Birds of prey and
Soars directly into the sun.
It is that bird with
The most bravery that has
The greatest wing span.
It is that bird with
The greatest intangibles that travels
The farthest distance.

Choke Ink

My mind rests in my hands
Like the world on the
Shoulders of storytellers.
My mind begs my hands for relief
Like weary heads pleading to the
Moon, beds, pillows and sheets
For therapeutic sleep.
I dream in ink,
Sleepwalking wrists and fingertips
Travel their way
Through white goose feathers
So as to not choke on the
Forgetfulness of morning.
I dream in ink,
My restless quill stains pages red
Like it was the pistol in my mouth,
Completely clearing the path for
The words stuck in my throat.

The Way Our Poems Change Us

I walk into a poem
Clenching a pencil
Like a dagger in my fist
In an effort to let go of my secrets.
I try to let these things go as
If they are right there in my palm,
And not in my soul,
But they live in there.

I leave my poems a different person,
Trembling hands, pencils snapped -
I am a nervous wreck when
Facing my past.
I am a fearful mess
But still I choose
To write my wrongs.

Tampering With Camp

All jokes aside,
All jokes should be left outside.
Some people ought to be sleeping
In tents that have been poorly-pitched under
Doomed, storm-ridden, skies.
In tense situations,
We assume insinuations
Can be marked as truth
But they actually entail
Deviations from the original tales.
Cliff hangers,
Belaying the ropes of the noose,
There's no parachute to safety,
No knife to be used to be cut loose.
Some say it was never their intention -
Some say their confessions in a booth,
If you choose to treat your Glorious Mountain
Like its foundation was fabricated on
Faulty building blocks,
Lies will leave your marriage
Like failed nose-dives or a cup of Scotch -
On the rocks.

City Boy

Open country is no place for a busy mind,
Where car horns sound,
A flurry of voices collide and
Stress hangs over heads like
A night of aiding sorrow.
Crowded cities clutter noises
Into every crevice of peace and Quiet.
Miles of rolling grass only
Filter fear from fleeing thoughts.
Open country reminds me
Of a heart that beats of boredom
Instead of frustrated passion,
A mind that is free of worry,
A soul comfortable without any
Experience of confrontation.
Open country is an escape
But it is not a solution.
I am a City Boy.
Open country is no place
For such a busy mind.
Open country should not invite
Guests of burdens.
Open country should know
Mixing stress and sleep is like an
Incestuous deed the way they surely seed death.
Open country couldn't resemble
My empty chest any more,
Open country couldn't distract me
From that fact any less.

The Innocence

In a plaid dress she stood,
Mostly, bold in her heroics.
Seven years of a troubling life and
She accepted the punishment
Of not turning in her assignment.
Her parents didn't help her make an effort,
They could only make her a
Target following their arguments.
Her hands may have held nothing,
It was something hard to present,
But had she rolled up her sleeves and
Lifted her dress,
The cuts and bruises would've made a
Hell of a Show-And-Tell.
That's why she preferred playing pretend.

The Youngest Courage

What is it that we knew as anxious Children,
What Wisdom have we left behind,
What Courage have we lost -
Playing in the rain was a
Hopeful Dream we carried,
To bathe in crystal droplets of the sky.
But now, we find reasons to shelter our skin
From the tears that drip from clouds.
What Courage have we lost that
We can not see the beauty of the storm.
What Courage have we lost that
We can not submerge our souls in deep
Freediving so as to dance
Within our own dirty puddles.
What Courage have we lost that
We can not immerse ourselves in allowing
Sunken ghost ships to surface.
What Courage have we lost that
We can not stare in our hearses,
Draw open our coffins and want
To play in the rain just once more.
I'd like to know,
What Courage have we lost?

Claustrophobia: A World That Isn't Big Enough For All Of Us

I gave up the gimmick of trying
To put a finger on what makes people tick,
To get my systematic hands on the answer.
The cogs that turn in revolutions
To ignite cognitive resolutions
Stand still turning stomachs.
The motives, like sprockets,
That cause them to act on
Their greed, actually shoot off
The rockets that Seek-and-destroy.
Let's go on a vacation free
From all the threats,
In exception to the occasional
Mauling by a Lion -
Even in paradise, lying shakes the
Business hand of risk and
Gambles with a pair of dice.
Let's go on an adventure,
Parting wild flowers and Exotic scents,
Kindling a fiery passion - like a
Drop of a match as it hits the gas -
When I lay you down on soft sands.
Gosh, it's taken me my
Whole life to get lost
And yet I'm,
Exactly,
Where I need to be.
Beside you.

I use to be afraid of the Life
I could be living before I met
The comforting security of your arms.
Let's pack our things, a permanent leave,
Far away from harm and the trespassings
That leave our souls in stress.
Let's go on a vacation so we may
Escape the rest of the World.
Those who argue that our worth is
Based off of our fine possessions and
The name we've made
Fail to see that the attention and time
They gave to fulfill those material dreams
Will leave an empty space in their
Graves that remain the same size as ours.
But the hours we spend are ours to
Try and haggle a profit.
Prophets and False idols
Hassle to force a belief,
Trying to sway the masses
To heed their warnings
That Sin defeats any chance
Of making it past the Golden Gates.
Doesn't that whole order seem out of place?
My mistakes are of no one's right to judge.
My mistakes are mine to be made.

I'm rich in my flaws
And the lessons I've learned.
I'm rich in my dreams
And the wisdom I've earned.

I'm rich in my ability to
Acknowledge right from wrong
And to tell when words are meant to
Be honest or deceitful.

I Turned this life I Live around;
I made a U-Turn away from Evil.

We have never taken a step back on
The progress we promised
Ourselves to reach for,
Despite those times that
Proved to be tough,
For after all, if the sky is truly our limit,
Haven't we been caged in enough?
Space and Stars -
We've been forsaken to touch.
Forget the age to come or pity things
We "have" to get done,
Open up your mind to the things
You were too blind or dumb
To realize and don't succumb
To the traps they've set.

July Twenty-Third

There was a Grand Welcoming
Parading across her lips.
Invitations to a show of fireworks,
Her lips bowed to me,
Her smile a sincere curtsy.
She was a well-mannered enigma.
She was the Life as if a Party.

When A Boy Says I Love You

The first time a boy says
He loves you, he will not know
How it is suppose to sound on his lips or
How it is supposed to choke in his throat.

The first time a boy says
He loves you, he will not know
His procrastinated efforts could cost
Him his chance of being with you, plus
All and the rest of his
Happiness from that moment on.

The first time a boy says
He loves you, he will not know
His voice will resonate in childish
Innocence one last time.

The first time a boy says
He loves you, he will not know
What exactly he is until
He speaks such words.

The first time a boy says
He loves you, he will not know
That because he
Wholeheartedly meant it,
He has taken the last step in
Becoming a real man.

The first time a boy says
He loves you, do not judge him
For having no grasp on the situation,
For how his eyes tremble in
Meeting yours like a timid pup,
For how he offers his condolences
For the awkwardness or
For how he doesn't directly follow with the
Best or most romantic of kisses under starlight.

The first time a boy says
He loves you, he is preparing himself
To confess that he is in love with you but
That is another step he will have to learn how
To take before it's made.

The first time a man says
He loves you,
Remember how he
Has learned to mean it.
The first time a man says
He is in love with you,
Remember how he
Has learned to value the
Sound of his words.

How You Make Love To A Woman

When I ask how do you love your woman,
I do not expect to hear
How you beat that up or
How you made her yours or
How you tore her clothes or
How you left it sore.

I do not expect to hear
How you told her to try new things or
How she screamed your name or
How you got your way or
How you claim your skills make her day.

When I ask how do you love your woman,
I do expect to hear
How you hold her hand or
How you make her understand your
Proud to be her Man.

I do expect to hear
How you hold her tight or
How she is your last thought and
    Every dream at night.

I do expect to hear
How you make sweet bare love,
But,
Please,
Spare the naked details.

I do expect to hear
How you lay afterwards and
Could talk forever, and
How that makes it all feel real.

I do expect to hear
How you are so fucking lucky
To have found a girl so
Willing to be hurt because..

..When I ask you
How do you love *your* Woman,
The thought of
Sex should come second,
The correction,
"My Goddess, you mean?"
Should come first.

Subconscious Consent

We all just want someone to
Read between our lines
But find ourselves stunned in awe,
Stunted in disbelief every time,
When someone can finish
Every one of our sentences.

We all just want for someone to
Ease our worried minds
But find it impossible for
Our magic tricks of
Masking our emotions
To be solved by any member
Of our audiences.

We all try to maintain that certain
Facade of mysterious composure
But just desperately want someone to
Peek behind the veil;
To be more concerned with the
Behind-the-scenes and curtain call.

Love wasn't meant to be a show of
Smoke and Mirrors,
Crystal Ball Foresight or
Tarot Cards and
Palm Readings.

It's uncomfortable to know that someone can
Decipher our thoughts and past so willingly.
It's understandable;
It's simply about the vulnerability.

If someone can pinpoint our every move,
Predict the person we are inside,
What's not to stop them from knowing
Exactly how to hurt us the most.

What we don't realize, however,
Is that when we're with the right person,
We let ourselves go free.
We subconsciously confess
Our trespassings and reveal the hearts
We wear under our sleeves,
Marked up by the filthy dirt,
Scabbed up blood and
The visually-displeasing s
Scars of bad healing.

What we mistake for clairvoyance,
              for mind-reading,
              for coincidence,
Is actually proof that someone will
Always find you interesting enough
So as to obsess over the challenge
Of knowing you better than
You will ever know yourself.
They pay attention and what that
Effort entails is, simply, True Love.

That's The Dream

Settling down o
On my first steps
Out of bed,
I find you
Beside me and
I'm living the dream.
Breaking from a
Sleepy slumber every morning,
Yet with eyes wide
I cycle through sights of certain fantasy -
Fragments of perfection
Sewn together so effortlessly
In a sequence that have become the
Bedazzled presence of your image.
I rise strong and steady with you like
The Moon and Stars behind
The high tide's full might.
I rise courageous and
Curious with you like
Gatherers in glory, Chiefs of a Tribe.
I look to you like a follower and
Up to you like a role model,
I turn to you for the answers and
Wear your name on my
Lips like my life's motto.
You're my heroine,
And here within,
I know I can tip toe up
The tallest mountains,

Scale the eldest trees,
Crawl across the
Broad shoulders of this planet and
Quench the thirst I
Accumulated by drinking
The oceans and seas with cupped hands.
I want to learn of your mind -
A library of who you are,
Take twenty books at a time
Off the shelves and
Spend hours studying until I
Know you better than yourself.
You've swept up the lingering mess I am,
Searching for the insight
Hidden behind the cobwebs.
You have a habit
Of rehabilitating hope
Into clarity of purpose.
Being with you,
Now, that's the dream come true.

Old Souls, Young Fun

Sun-burnt cheeks and dirty faces,
Bumper cars and haunted mansion mazes,
Ferris wheel romance,
Hearts like roller coaster rides racing -
In the dizziest of places,
The girl who drives me crazy
Proves to be the
Prized Possession
My heart won't stand to
Have pried from its possession
Because even on the fair grounds
I won't fight on fair ground
To hold on to the one person
That makes sense of
Life's Merry-Go-Rounds and
Makes merry feelings go around.
I swear, every ride that's
Thrown me down and
Stolen my equilibrium
Has been no match for the
Girl who is my Balance.

Lottery

I am like a child.
I am spoiled -
How you read
My mind,
It's like
We're synchronized.
Your ability to
Decipher my needs,
Nonpareil.
Though, I'm sorry,
I'm selfish
To always expect it.

Once Crumbled, Now Golden

Even Gilded hearts have known
The Beautiful sorrow of past war-torn love.

Nova Altitude

Bright by birthright,
You cannot keep me caged
Anymore than you can
Keep the Sun from rising.

Temple and Vessel

The oldest wisdoms came at the youngest patience.
The purest peace was born from the busiest silence.

Whistles

Words and Quills met
Paper like Wind to
Arrows and Quivers,
Warriors with a message.

Grand Illusionist

I was conscious of the
Consequence of confidence.
Where intellect and disrespect
Intersect, I interjected the
Indirect connection was incorrect
In its ways to intercept accomplishments.
I was a narcissist abusing the cartridges
Of an arsonist dressed in dissonance.
Pairs of lies paralyzed my friendships.
I was forbidden from the formalities of
Salutations and thus singled-out
For being forsaken.
I was an example of what an
Exile-slash-Exhibitionist looked like.
I was a disciple of emergency exits,
A grand illusionist.

For Sake Of Solving Forsaken Puzzles

I've seen the likes of many miles,
Days in to long days out
But I've never been so
Amazed by anything else
As the way your eyes
Travel to meet mine
With forgiveness and
Expend valuable time
To learn what I'm about.

This will be our longest journey,
As you try to wrap your head
Around my mysteries.
You've never prayed for time
To slow nor stop but instead,
Altogether, dismiss it,
For the sake of solving this puzzle.

Letters: Part V

Hello and Good Morning,
I hope that you slept well.
I hope you raised
Not a tad bit tired
At the ringing of your alarm's bell.
I hope you're ready to
Face this cruel world -
The challenges it has planned ahead
Serve as no will-breaker
For the girl who will not tire
Even when out of breath.
Darling, I hope that you wake up
With the plans of
Learning from my mistakes and
That you understand the
Game Life plays,
Take and Take.
We're still expected to give.
Turn the tables in your favor -
Do what you must but don't give in.
Take chances,
And take those who oppose you
And take you for granted
And have mercy on those fools instead.
Be successful and happy on your own accord,
My friend, that is the best revenge.
The World is yours for the taking, my Queen.
My Honor kneeling at your feet,
My Loyalty in your hands.

Letters: Part VI

I really hope that you know
I'm so far in Love with You that
I'll never find my way back out;
For that matter,
I'd have it no other way.

Unsent Letters: Part II

I admire your determination
To get all the things that you must done.
I admire all of your effort
To make sure every battle is won.
I love how you fight
For what you believe in and
How you're still learning what that is.
I love that you're not power-hungry
Or money-burning
But instead, you quench
Your thirsts with knowledge.
It drives me crazy when you look at me,
Eyes wide or squinting.
It drives me crazy when you hold me,
My eyes cry and thoughts flourish
Out from the chambers that
Have trapped me;
(But that you barged down and opened)
Now, I'm finally at peace with
Myself, my flaws, mistakes and transgressions.
I love how you know me
And how you've let me love you.
I love how the fact that I know it's
Real brings me to tears around you;
How I can let my sorrows flow
Out from my mouth
Instead of my wrists,
How you kiss my lips with a healing potion
That sweeps the need to intentionally let

The red blood spill into a mess and contains
The hurt with soul-sheathing bandages.
I've learned that now that I'm with you
I've grown more afraid of the world.
Two people out of thirteen billion
And you're the one that I found?
How'd a Goddess end up with a Clown?
I suppose opposites attract,
And, well, I've always been a jokester.
I wouldn't have a shot without you -
You're the pistol to my holster.
I need you to understand that while
I aim to hold up you,
I always meant to do this,
That is,
To heart-rob you, Heartthrob.

Just A Reminder

I Love You
First and Foremost.
Remember that
Whenever, Wherever
And for Whatever
Reason you find trouble.
I am always here for you.
Don't ever pass on the security
Of knowing that you have me
For the rest of my days.
You have rightfully claimed
My heart as your own.
Our hearts, as two, beat as one.
My ears will always listen to you;
Your worries,
The details of your days
And
The long stories of
The memories from your past.
My eyes and hands
Will always search for you,
Even under the veil of dark times.
My feet will always climb on your heels,
Following the long shadow of your footsteps.
My soul will continue to
Playfully waste the years
By and by with yours -

An Ancient Love that has
Walked along the
Tides of time
And
Sculpted the very
Masterpiece of
The "Perfect Love"
That others strive
So hopefully to capture
In words, paintings, actions
And inside of their own hearts.

The Only Soul Left Unscathed

She wasn't just a bombshell.
Even under pressure,
She showed more substance
In the conviction condensed
In the stride of her strut.
My eyes took her abstract aesthetics
In like an addiction;
Like lungs inhaling the chemicals
Unfiltered by the cigarette butt.
She was dangerous;
One single touch could have your hands
Smoking like a freshly fired gun.
She was perfection:
Eyes of fire set to ignite her life's aspirations,
Her dowsing pendulum curves could make
Any man a slave under their control,
Subtle skin, luscious lips, hypnotizing hips -
When all these things materialized,
You may have wondered if, in fact,
The Devil was in disguise.
She was the vixen of rebellion rule,
        The harbinger of fresh perfume,
            Used to coat her fiery fumes,
        The jaw-dropper that, consequently,
            Made men spew drool,
        The Goddess of potential and challenge,
            Defied the fixed odds,
            Shattered the dice and
            Made fools of the men that watched on.

Her wits outplayed the sharpest of minds,
She loved being pushed to the edge;
Her strategy was playing from behind.
Your hope would meet its demise,
Her blades would catch your back
With ease every time;
An Olympic Ice skater teasing the skills of
An imprudent idiot treading thin ice.
Sporting such raw natural beauty
Has become the modern controversy -
Since when has it been okay to be
Completely comfortable with yourself?
She was the last soul dancing within the fire.
Reborn at every turn, spin and leap,
Eyes closed not because
She ever feared the dark but
Because she found herself
Free from harm
After she set herself
At peace, with herself.

Trials To Tame

Instead of moving mountains for me,
Let us climb the heights and
Scale their immensity down in our power
While challenging the thousands of faces
Of resetting suns to stare-downs.
Instead of killing yourself for me,
Relive every day with me and
When our time comes,
Let rebirth sweep through our throats.
Otherwise, of my loss,
What will I become?
Instead of giving up everything for me,
Become my all and everything but please,
Remember of how I am kneeling and
Begging please,
Don't you ever, ever, ever, give up on me.

It's Only In My Nature To Love

I just need a little taste of honey.
Honestly, temptation runs wild.
I know you're busy,
You'll always be working, but
Take some time off to
Warm me in the spring.
It's been a long winter and
I have so much love to bare.
It's only in my nature.
I only want to hibernate
With a heart and stomach
Filled with your love.

Long Walks Through The Park With Philophobia

I had become my own therapist,
Treating my emotional issues with
Straight, warm, whiskey shots
Poured into decorative porcelain teacups.
Eventually, I found, I thought
It would be a great idea to
Close my eyes and walk
Through the crowded park
To see how far I got
By trusting myself.
Dizzy enough to stumble
Like a poor drunken fool,
My feet followed one after the other,
Like the shots from earlier that
Afternoon that had gone down smooth.
At first, it seemed crazy.
It was a terrifying thing to
Never see it coming at all.
I bumped into something tall,
Unlike a wall, it was soft and caught me,
Held me and helped me,
Asked me if I was okay
And as I looked up to unveil the beautiful face
That stood gleaming in grace -
That was the moment I learned they were wrong
About the motions of the myth they spoke of.
Who ever said you had to actually fall
The moment you stood falling in Love?

Steadfast

Your success isn't an expectation.
It's the belief I have that you'll
Always conquer whatever it is you apply
Your skills, abilities and mind to.
I believe in you, and,
In the power of you.

It's Easy To Love You So

When you are crying,
Which for sake of my sinking heart
I hope is never,
I will always bare the reassurance
Confirming that everything will be okay.

When I need you dearly,
Which in this case you must
Know is always,
I'd never depart from your arms.

As I had wasted away
Until the very day we met,
You must remember
You are my greatest adventure.
You are my grandest fear.
You have the entire pile of my
Years in sand trickling
Through your fingers,
My heartbeat sitting in
Your hourglass hands.

When you hold me,
Hold me tight as you would
The walls of the sand sculptures
You'd build on the beach.

Do not hold me loose with
Rustling wrists if you can not resist
Dribbling my time into sloppy drip castles.

Love me true,
Create me a freedom,
Make me stand tall
Against the waves and
I will hold your spine,
Support your neck and
Have your back,
Against the most troubling winds.

Atone

If I ever do you wrong,
Won't you, please, let me atone.
I do not think we will fair well
When we are all alone;
Together, we can have it all,
The good, the bad, and
Still survive the fall,
Get up bruised and
Harmed, but,
In one piece and
Yet very much alive.

Worries aside,
Loving you leaves
No room for
Mistakes or lies.

Crisp Leaves

And in the sky,
Our branches will grow.
Long roots like fingers,
Our hands that hold,
Onto each other,
Overlap and grasp tight,
Sturdy bases for a connection,
Reaching to Outer Spaces,
Stars dangling from our Love,
Like Summer's Peaches.
A taste of our love,
Cosmic and corrosive,
Powerful and potent,
A love for the ages,
A Sacred nature unfazed
By the surrounding Wildfires,
Incombustible to the flames of
Envy's untamed hatred.

The Vices Of Asking Axes For Advice

Revealing the zeal for Setting Suns,
We conceal the appeal of shooting the
Moon down with hands shaped like guns.

When new days are promised and
Beds creak under our weight,
Lead heads label dismissal of opportunities
As avoiding the possibility of mistakes.

We are knee deep in concrete only
Because we placed our feet there first.

If fists could speak,
Ours would beg and plead
To swing at our own cheeks
If only to make the thought of it hurt.

Clouded and misguided,
Quitting has become our lightning response,
We appear for an instance,
Then doors slam like thunder
When we've abandoned hope and gone.

Our thoughts can be heard through
Cataracts and Bulwarks
But we ignore these great ideas that
Rudely knock our tempos with forceful impact
As we're too busy running into walls.

Reckless and selfish,
Defenseless in brashness,
Our roots and branches have
Grown feeble and defective.

Delicate like precious porcelain,
Our petite perseverance
Cracks and crumbles under pressure;
Pitiful presences just
Aren't worth a pretty penny.

The Reasons We Read

Every part of a story
Modestly basked in its climax,
Like a Peacock fanning its
Elaborate iridescent coloration
Adorned upon its tail feathers.

In comparison to the problematic plot
That was the life I longed to escape,
Any stories sequenced coherently enough
Were good enough to distract
My worried mind,
My somber soul.

Books saved me;
Their playful imagery shapeless
Until met with the hands behind
This thick skull.

They would mold me into the
Hero of foreign lands,
A protagonist heralding the
Defeat of iniquitous circumstance,
But, sometimes,
I was the Malevolent Lunatic,
A malicious antagonist practicing heresy
Against the righteous path.

Stories showed me I'm not the only
Author needing to assert some revision,
That I wasn't the only one writing a sad story
But instead of playing pretend with the vision
Of where I was headed,
That I should focus more on
Seeking the truth behind
My starving, carving instead of crying,
For My own happy ending.
Dig deep,
The reasons we read are exactly
The reasons we write.

Crop Circles

You left me frozen,
Exiled to the fields where
Generations feed,
Crushed and battered,
Bruised and scattered,
Left for dead,
So badly beat,
I fell for your mysterious ways
Of revealing the mysteries and
Grand plot of the Universe.
You stole me from the
Only ground I've ever known,
And, though dirty and chaotic,
Unpraised and ravaged by man,
My realm was the one place I called home.
My head, my reality,
The hymns I sung in my mind,
Replaced with your whispers,
Silent sinister snickers,
Chuckles of a child that's
Cheated to ensure a
Checkers or chess game win
But grins, "Your Turn!"
All because they know
They're ten paces ahead.
The spaces, a drop off,
Miles between us,
A disconnect that turns off
The comfortable feeling and

Toggles on the uneasy queasiness
Of realizing the dangers of
Sleeping with my enemies that are
Tucked inside the impression
Of what my idea of myself ought to be.
You showed me the height and reach of the world,
If opportunities stood in closing doors,
I'd slam the poor excuse of a wood board,
Just to burn the house to the floor.
I've broken from my tendencies,
Yearned to be engulfed by possibilities,
Extended far past my spiritual zone of serenity,
Just so my bones could speak
Loudly of the way I used
To let the weight of my burdens
Dictate my progress and
Selfishly hide away.
You probed my problems,
Tested my touchy heart,
Ran exams of my vitals
And kept my self-worth
Bottled up the day you
Put me on a shuttle to depart
Like a message sent in a
Glass boat to embark.
When you abducted me,
I suppose it was all in your nature,
You were the other ten percent of me that
My mother's hope for me nurtured.
By the time I drifted back down and
Returned to my reality,

My island had grown more
Proportional and stable,
There was no need to see a shrink.
I was driven mad by hesitation,
I was smudging the edges of an
Oil-painting Master-piece with the
Worry constructed from imaginary creation.
Even Crop Circles have their explanations.
Though doubt couldn't grant me answers,
It delivered the indirect results of
Living in the present knowing
Life is all a lesson.
I won't shy away from what's been given.
I'll glisten as long as I aim to
Be silent;
I've arranged to listen.

Nights

Blank canvases, our bodies,
Skies curious to know what stars are.
Cue our clenched eyes to open wide
So they may burn like Suns.
Let the constellations reveal themselves
From the sparks of our lips and
Fire of our loins.
Let stars shift, nebulae form,
Dust settle, galaxies calm, and
Scientists and philosophers begin
To try to begin to define or
Theorize the power of this
Big Bang.

Arms Like Iron Maidens

She was falling in love with me and
I was fearing the moment I would have to catch her.
My arms were curses,
Doomed and riddled
With malevolent dangers.
Makeshift Iron Maidens turned One
Innocent by-stander to the
Definition of the standard martyr.
I guiltily sat back to witness my
Heart strike at her
"I love you" like it was
The tripwire for a
Conspiring Venus flytrap.
I realize that I have got
More than I'll ever need,
For she, still, walks well beyond
The realm of torture.
She kisses black holes and, somehow,
They turn to the hearts
Of nebulae and galaxies.
Trust may take time but
Courage takes longer,
She finds her own
Guilty pleasure in harnessing the
Ways to alchemize
The greatest of weaknesses into
The most ultimate of powers.

Dam, That's Deep

Beautiful music spilled from her mouth as
She filled me with her deepest secrets.
I was something once defined by its constant volume,
Teeny-tiny and Minuscule, and now,
I stood in the literal perspective of
Seeing the glass as half full.
She read to me the volumes of encyclopedias
That charted her past.
She was the Siren of the Floodgates,
Singing to me my happy ending.
The walls she built to hold back her
Reservoir of tears would
Only hear the last letter
She ever read to me.
She hit her final note -
Au Revoir.
She crashed into my arms.
There was a beauty in the practicality
Of giving yourself to someone in your entirety.
I accepted the weight of the waves she came with
And I drowned happily in easing her sorrows.

The Reacher

I sail into the soft veil of
Slumberous swoons when
I cuddle you, my little spoon.
At times of resting,
The sound of shallow breaths
Set my worries to bed
So I may drift into
Blankets of cashmere sand.
Your lungs hum like waves
In their rise-and-fall
In such a way the sequence
Silences my troubles.
I do not deserve this sanctuary
But your heart casts my mind to sleep
So dreams may carry me to another day.
Your breaths, Oh,
How they heal the weary.

The Settler

Passing a hand over your Moons,
I polish them with the seal of curiosity.
Chasing the harvest of your Winter and Springs,
I incant prayers to enchant
Your chances of succeeding.
I wish nothing but the best for you.
I am a native sorcerer but also a javelin thief.
I have roamed the same realm for many years,
Riding the impact others have had,
Hunting and reaping the
Results like they're my own.
You are a time traveler but also a stubborn fool.
You have always made time a pressing issue,
Buckling in and pushing forward,
Achieving more in seven days than
Most do in their entire lives since the
First breath they took when they were born.
Yet, you found something in the
Washed-out pale blue of my eyes..
Yet, you found something in the
Fading warmth of my touch..
Yet, you found something in the
Stone-cold breath of my frail lungs..

I have roamed the same realm for many years,
Searching for an escape.

You have rushed through time's trials in hopes
Of finding life's answers.

It seems,
We both have found
Our purpose,
Our calling.

My Settler, I love you, if only,
For making home of my aching heart.

Hex

Compatible mindsets,
Vulnerable necks and
Backs scratched.
Incredible sex,
Best friends and
Climax.
A good nights rest,
Pacing downtown streets
Holding hands.
Tomorrow, we'll race back to bed.

Nemesis

How good rivals evil and
Light battles dark;
Complimentary elements,
Cigarettes -
Dark tar
Playing hide-and-seek with a
Piezoelectrical spark.
Pick your poison and
Make it your obsession.
Any other day,
I'd be your end;
I'd take you down,
I'd take you out.
But, tonight,
I'll keep both my
Friends and enemies closer
Than any other.
Tonight,
I'll take you out.
Later,
Tonight,
I'll take you down.

Phoenix

What wicked weapon do you wield,
What witchery wraps around my
Dead judgment that you may
Turn me from dust to flesh?
Revive me in a second's flash
With the first and only kiss, I'll ever cherish.
Manipulated muscles, like a marionette,
It's child's play how my body
Feels like it is operating
Behind the blushing emotions
That sprung from the touch of our hands.
You liven me.
Your breaths swell the lungs hung
On the gallows inside my rib cage and
Fills the heart in my chest with
The valor to escape the treacherous noose.
Love – a curse?
Love, a spell aged to perfection
To preserve the quality of real connections.
Love, the traveling fountain of youth.

Frostwalker

A crystalline moon of amethyst
Sits silently in the violaceous scenery
Stretching across the
Twilight of the Tundra.
Isles imbued with the
Magic of malachites
Call to the glaciers
Garnished entirely
In rugged garnet stones.
Frostwalkers wade through the
Spectral souls of
Tourmaline trees that
Once combed the clouds.
Eyes like aquamarine stones glow,
Alive in the candlelight
Blazing like the dancing amber
Collected from ancient arbors.
She was ultraviolet rays
Searing the deepest depths of
My heart with her initials.
She was infrared light
Guiding my path safely
While warming me
Skin to bone to soul.

Skypouncer

Feline footwork made light
Of the fine lines we learn to walk.
Her paws so nimble she didn't
Need nimbus clouds to pounce upon,
She was comfortable leaping her way
Through the traps threading together
Ambitiously driven and Absolutely mad.
She triangle jumped her way through
The skyscrapers and trees that climbed the
Heights of heavens knowing
She was the Queen Lioness of passion, that
She was the High Empress of aspirations.
She pushed her natural abilities
Outside the reach of her usual habitat and,
That is why,
She stands bloodied but unbroken.
She lives like there is,
But one life to triumph
The value of having nine.

Tangerine Mint Gimlets

I admire the way you've stolen
My technique;
Rolling my own thick
Lower lip between yours,
Biting down with the intention
Of intense, passionate, pain and
Finishing with a nibble
Softer than a Guppy's and
A peck softer than a Dove's.

I admire the way you
Stare into my eyes and
How you piercingly peer
Through the expressions
On my face like
Windows with their
Curtains drawn back and
Leer upon my naked, seduced, mind.

I admire how you know that the
Very first touch and
Very last thrust
Captures the state of
Awe your body puts me in:

It starts with a smile,
Recoil and wrinkles around
The corners of my eyes.

It ends with an innocent
Drop of the jaw,
Relief in the tension of
My eyebrows and toes,
And
Sends shivers through
My fragile glass being.

Tender

There was a silence
In the way she moved.
There was a silence
In the way she breathed.
There was only silence
Like the way my Secrets
Hushed the rest of my existence to
Slumber beneath sheets and
Blankets of my skin.
Never did she let out a scream,
She knew her way around
My rough rugged edges
Like she was the
Caretaker of my Ancient corridors.
She accepted when I'd turn to run.
She accepted when I'd slam my doors.
She took quiet steps so as
To not disturb my rest.
She accepted that I expected
Never to be seen again,
With no exception when
Given the chance to flee.
She made home of my
Abandoned facility and
Kept it as it was,
Finding comfort in
All the sharp turns.

My walls trembled there in ruin,
They've piled rubble far
Too high to see it all topple.
She put a hand on the solid granite
Of my floors, and,
Though she knew all about the
Hidden passages and
Maze-like labyrinths and
All the places to hide,
She thought it was time to
See my true face.
She prepared for the difficult task
Of dropping the biggest bomb
In the softest of ways,
Carefully, almost surgically,
She mouthed "I'm in love with you"
So it danced, momentarily, in my ears
Like the sound of a pin dropping on
The bricks stained with my tears.
There was a silence
In the way she stood so still.
Patient, she has never wanted to disturb me.
There was a silence
In the way walls came crumbling down.

Sundays

She turned her hands
To hold my own and
Told me it's okay.
"You're no cursed soul for
The ways you tried to
kill your pain and sadness."

The Teachings Of A True Father

She wasn't born behind walls built by
Promises of princes and prosperity.
She was raised by the bed time
Tales of magic and the gift of the
Guidelines her Father gave her
For recognizing the True Love she deserved.
She, in that sense, was rich,
Not in gold but a life's lessons and secrets.

Unconquerable

I never wanted to burden
Your mind with the expectations
I lay on its shoulders.

I never wanted to prove to be an obstacle
You'd have to go out of your way for.

I never wanted to make you feel
That you always had to behave certain ways
Around me or hide certain emotions or truths.

I never wanted someone as perfect as you.
Truth is,
I've never deserved it.

You're not perfect, by its own definition,
But in my mind,

You've always epitomized my idea of it.

I never wanted to just wake up beside you.

I've always wanted
To never have to
Leave your side -
To wake up,
Live our days
One by one and go to bed,
Hand-in-hand.

But for now, for it's all I can do,
I want to climb up your spine,
Tuck my body in the comfort of yours,
Hide my face in the cave where
The edge of your neck meets your shoulder,
And, while grasping your left breast in
My left palm, as if it could ever be your heart,
Let my whispers carry through your ears:

"I'm so impressed by all you do,
So proud of all you've accomplished and
So obsessed with the determination
Buried in your heart.
I'm proud of the person you've always been."

Royalty In Nosebleed Seats

She never expected to bathe in Gold,
Take first-class trips around the Globe,
Have endless money to blow,
Egyptian cottons and Cashmere clothes,
Hands filled with rings of gems and precious stones
Or necklaces of time-perfected pearls.

She just wanted a man who was
A Lover not a Fighter but
Fought for what he Loved.

It had never been about securing herself a
Fool wealthy in possessions.
She craved Knowledge and Real experiences;
Not half-there moments with washed-up has-beens.

She just wanted a best friend with
Whom to adventure.

It wasn't about power, opportunity or
A life free of worry.

She just wanted a man who could
Prove he'd be worthy of her Love and Time.

She only needed a man with a Lion's Heart,
Whose claws were bony, bloodied, knuckles and
Whose roars were warnings he made sure
Everyone heard – he was hers.

She only needed a man with promise,
And, Together,
[We] found bliss.

Cease The Day, Carpe Noctem

I shot for the stars in such a literal sense,
Carpe diem didn't expect me to seize the day
By wrangling its neck with my own two hands.
It's ironic the way day light was mourning
After I put its sun down.

Conducting Chaos

Possibilities and doubts collide
Behind the veil of our dreams,
Portrayed like clouded horizons.
Conflicts of stormy skies bicker and
Raise their outraged voices,
Matching fist-for-fist in a
Show of dominance:
Booms of Thunder,
Boons of Lightning flashes.
The light shed brings rise,
Like morning, to my best efforts.
Men with hopes for the throne,
Like No-Man's land,
May storm the castle,
For claim of a place uneventful,
I'll Storm the Skies to
Show the Stars
All the reasons to be fearful.

Only If I Tremble

Should my words fumble over the
Edge of my tongue's tip,
Should my hands gloss over
With sweat and nervousness,
Should I lose control over my frozen body
That has grown tense,
Should my heart race in my chest like a lap
With a pure rush of adrenaline,
Should my mind travel through the pulses of
Possibilities of any effect that you may have in my
life,
Should my entire existence shutter at the
Thought that luck could make you my wife,

I would know almost automatically and
Surrender myself immediately and willingly
To the purpose of dedicating my time to orbit yours,
So you know that the dance we sway to
Through the endless moments of
Calm quietness in your room
Gives me goosebumps because
I'm in love with you so deeply and
Though I stand unsteady on my axis,
You correct my perspective,
Become my balance and together,
Our bond is as permanent,
Strong, as gravitational pull.

The Lights Tremble

When I miss you, the
Lights tremble as they already know
They should start closing their eyes.

The way my fingers itch to
Climb your spine,
My thighs fiending to rub
Electrifying friction against yours,
The world really has no clue
What happens behind our closed doors.

I absolutely need to leave hickies
Streaked across your chest,
Fresh gashes down your ribs and back,
And blood bruises from where my
Hands owned your ass.

I absolutely need to be beside you,
Devouring your flesh with the
Lust of my pounding heart.

You are my sexy little vixen and
I absolutely need to pull your hair and
Yell how much I need you and love you,
And only you.

When I miss you, the
Lights tremble watching the
Powerful and passionate love we make.

When I miss you, our
Energies shatter reality,
Lending personification to inanimate objects
Through the thrusts and quakes,
Because,
Even the lights can not stop staring,
Though,
I would not have that kink
Any other way.

Serpentine Skylines

The sky sheds its skin so as to serenade
The orisons of those whose origin
Root directly from the shades
Of blue and silver waves.
Scales, both altocumulus and cirrocumulus,
Slide across the azure scenery much as
Snakes slide like silk over the
Touch of bare earth.
Empyrean cymbals sing to celestial bodies
As serpentine skylines
Wind around the Sun.
Heavenly reign of sapphire afternoons
Make sanctuary of sands and seas alike.
Rain fills fields and still
Awe captures us like
Willing victims.

Incandescence

Inventors.
We're bright minds sidelined by our closed eyes.

Rattled by lessons of keeping
Our heads screwed on tight,
We've trapped our inspirations
In glass-dome cages,
Windows to the World -
Presenting our spark,
Containing our spirit.

We've learned to never give our ideas
A chance to be carried away,
To never let them drift free of weight,
Buoyant in the clouds like sky lanterns.

Instead we compromise them,
Fooled by the illusion of endless
Tomorrows promised to come,
We postpone the thoughts
We should draw action from and
Never really start or get the job done.

Procrastination rearranges our priorities,
Gutting the organs
For the satisfaction of the
Sounds of groans.

We mustn't take any shortcuts
Around short circuits.

We must surge to free our troubled Souls.

Smoke rises through like distress signals
To let us know sometimes
Fuses are meant to be blown,
So we may draw focus from the shadows.

Horizons Drawn Like Henna

Horizons drawn like Henna,
Last breathes like
Spiraling mists of
Diamond dust,
Stars never streamed like
Strung pearls until today.

Hand-to-hand combat never seemed
To swing and dip like
A romantic dance
But today it's our ambitions
Inhabiting our movements.

Oceans never claimed to
Repair the lost
Or baptize the broken but
When dragging us under we
Learned that the
Surmounting pressure is
The force that could
Forge fires as our ashes
Turned to phoenixes that
Could breathe water.

Evaporating the weight of w
Waves until the
Reach of courage
Empowered our wings,
Today, it's about our passion.

Today, we can sing of how
We can engulf setting suns at the
End of rivers of time and
At the farthest reaches of the sea
If only to remember that the hardest part of
Keeping pace with the horizon
Is bringing that same
Blazing desire and respect
To the furnace pulsing
Inside of our chests.
We are Horizons drawn like Henna,
Elegant existence stained shortly in skin,
Confounding courage embedded within
Our eyes,
Our souls,
Our fists.

Feathered Moon

We stitched the night with silver string
Like our thumbs were chelicerae,
Our fingers, eight spider legs,
Our wrists, the spinnerets spinning
Spools of crochet thread,
Our heads, the moon.
We crowned our skulls
With the actions of our bare hands,
Feathered Moons catching the
Fire of the futures,
Headdresses of sacred Charms,
Adornments of hallowed heritage.
We stitched the night with silver string
Hoping our foresight could prove right and
Guide the best of dreams to reality
Like Lighthouses or the North star
Beckoning lost ships at sea to
Safety of the shore's coast.
We stitched the night with silver string
Like spiders,
Capturing stars in our silk
So our web of opportunity
Could shine brightly
Through the deepest of sleep.
We stitched the night with silver string.
We sewed dreamcatchers along
The edges of the willow trees high above.
We made a mosaic galaxy of dreams.

Shattered Suns

Sandstorms couldn't stun my eyes.
I skipped shattered suns
Like smooth stones across
The sky laced with
Lakes of ice.
I sipped the nectar from
My broken days like
Island fruits.
I skipped shattered suns
Like smooth stones so
The sound of my memories
Could make the music
My muse would
One day dance to.
Time, itself, took notes
On how to cheat Death.
I put my hands on rising suns,
Held them and taught them,
I will always have skipped shattered suns.

Accuracy

Life was just an empty word
Our actions gave guts to.
Life was just an open wound
Our experiences let salt and remedies into.
Life was just an unused canvas
Our passion brushed colors and
Ambition's streaks through.
Life was just an unanswered question
Our curiosity and courage will always
Find ways of providing the answers to.
Life was just the bullet,
Our hands, the chamber it peers through.
The combination made the gun,
Our births were the loading, cocking and aiming.
Draw the breath and hold...
    ...You decide when it's time to shoot.

Purposeful Impact

Though a focus of intense daydreaming
Settles in over my Antique Globe,
The world I see sitting in front of me
Is realistically far from reach -
But a world closer than ever to being that of my own.

Scaling instances of existence down
To one-dimensional Maps,
It's easy using them as place mats
When glasses of water get knocked over
To bring life to the printed coasts,
A tidal wave of diffused ink,
Shark attacks that have bloodied my cove.

The calm of the storm follows
Where waves waltz and roll,
Now thoughts gently sway, cleansing
The edge of my skull; the
Sounds of the rhythm of deep breathing
Make paradise of this atoll.

Many travel, few survive the Journey if at all,
When turning their motivations from simple desire
Into lists of life's goals made possible.

Change will shape this world as
Ideas will color it in within the lines,
Breath-taking scenery will open eyes
The same way ancient wisdom opens minds.

My index finger crashed on the locations
Of my dream vacations
Like asteroids falling through Earth's atmosphere.

Curiosity and Inspirations,
Intentions and Aspirations alike, Combined,
Leaving maps with scattered targets,
Plans of hitting them all at a single time,
Having a blast with this life of mine.

So while airplanes get flown,
People learn to grow,
But the places where I aim to go
Will only add plenty of
Ammunition of experiences to
This shotgun soul.

Rough Roses

Flowers rose from her
Every open wound,
Every place where there was room
Resembled gorgeous gardens.
Her delicate petals were nothing
To underestimate.
I wonder if, perhaps,
She knew that even thorns,
Have their roses.
She wore thorns like they
Were stitched together
As a floral dress
Gleaming in the fairest shade
Of natural beauty.

Cinnamon Oceans

Here we stand neck-deep in Cinnamon Oceans.
Time carelessly passes over us like
Waves drowning desperate drifters for fun.
Here we stand, burying our heads in the
Sands that have seared our throats -
Branding the tests we tell stories of into our esophagi,
Inscriptions of our ghostly voices made
Designs to be laid into our sarcophagi.
Here we stand, Masochists to the cause,
Punching ourselves in the gut so as to
Vomit a reminder of
What it is like to cough up blood
From half-healed scars.
Here we stand, Freckle-stained faces,
Children blemished by the lessons of life and
Signatures of each unique sun ray -
Proof that time, both, wounds and heals.
Here we stand, caught in the Mouth of the Hourglass,
Unsure whether to be the horse-pill
That instills the fear of swallowing the fall
Or to let ourselves be crushed and gnashed,
Masticated to a point of no return.
Here we stand in Cinnamon Oceans,
A few bad decisions away from going under because
We are too ill-prepared to get over
The empty-headed errors.
Here we stand in Cinnamon Oceans,
Given a chance to unearth our lost bones
From the ruins yet to be excavated.

Here we stand in Cinnamon Oceans,
Hoodwinked by our own curiosity,
Hoaxed by our own brash bravery,
Handed over by the weakness in our Hearts,
Betrayed by the flaws that makes us,
All, perfectly human,
We have never had a fair shot
At making time our own.

We can say we beat the buzzer,
We can say we killed some time,
We can say we threw clocks out of the window,
We can say we have seized the day,
That this day is mine,
But while we chaunt our chauvinistic chimes
Of how we got our minute hands
To own the hour hands of time,
It silently enslaves our minds and
Assassinates us from behind the obsession,
As the therapeutic sessions of condemning
The counting cadence comes down to
Drowning it out by
Conducting the Orchestra of our last breaths.
Here we stand in Cinnamon Oceans,
Granted the choice to sink or swim
In the bodies of water made of our own decisions.
Here we stand in Cinnamon Oceans,
Galvanized by the same searing sand to sail,
To continue gallantly gallivanting around the globe,
Instead of haunting the taunting hourglass,
Regardless of how daunting the task may seem.

Special Thanks

*To The First Person To
Realize My Potential
And Help Guide Me
Through All The
Trials Of Flame And Time.*
Jen Varela*,
I Will Always Owe You Immensely
For The Hope And Pride
You Have Invested In Me.
You Are The Only Thing
In My Life That I Can Recognize
As My Single Most
Inspiring Muse.*

*And To All Those In My Life
From Whom I Gather
The Courage and Inspiration
For Creating My Art.*

Copyright © 2015 Jorge Andres Rodriguez
All rights reserved.
ISBN: 1499104545
ISBN-13: 978-1499104547

Made in the USA
Columbia, SC
15 October 2022